Underwater Bahamas
ISBN 99915-3-016-9
Library of Congress Catalog Card No. 92-062072

Published by Novelty Printers & Publishers
M. Utility, Male' 20-01, Republic of Maldives
Tel: 322490, 327041. Fax: (960) 327039. Telex: 66045 Novelty MF.

Represented in North America and Caribbean by:
Blue Edge Publications
P. O. Box 190213
Miami Beach, FL 33119
Phone/Fax: (305) 673-4069

CONTENTS

FOREWORD

Many people have been of great help to me on this book. My good friends at Novelty Publishing: Ali Hussein, Ismail, Asad, Asraf and Shahina, have been there since the beginning and given me the support needed to complete the project. I thank Ahmed Shakir for his precise work on the layout of the book. The Bahama diving community has been very helpful and I've found their operations to be uniformly excellent. Among them I'd like to especially thank: Stuart Cove of Stuart Cove's in Nassau, John Englander, Chris Allison, Ollie, Bert, Jan and the rest at UNEXSO in Lucaya, Dick Birch and the Small Hope Bay family on Andros, Bill and Nowdla Keefe from Bimini Undersea Adventures, Keith Rogers at Dive Abaco in Marsh Harbour, Brendal and Mary Stevens from Brendal's Dive Shop on Green Turtle Cay, Peter Kuska and Joerg Friese from Stella Maris Long Island and Tom Guarino and the crew of Sea Fever out of Miami Beach. I'd also like to thank: Paula Hayes of the Lucayan Beach Resort and Casino, Mike Kaboth of the Bimini Big Game Fishing Club, Ossie Brown of Compleat Angler fame, Ossie Hall of the Conch Inn Resort in Marsh Harbour and the Green Turtle Club and Marina, all for their hospitality. Earl Miller of The Bahamas Tourist Office and Sandy McDougle and Woody Wilson of Bahamasair all gave their support to the project and helped where they could. Robert Quintana and Beuchat lent their support and equipment. Nelson Marti of Bubbles Dive Center in Miami was a big help and a good friend. Linda Picula of the NOAA library on Virginia Key tracked down information and satellite photos. Many thanks to Doug Perrine for advice, consultation and strange food. Thanks Tim Friel for guarding my butt on a wild shark dive. Thanks as well to the Perrone family who not only allowed me but encouraged me to throw Donna in with the sharks.

The text of this book, poor grammar and all, has been my responsibility. Any mistakes in fact are my own unless someone else would like to take the credit.

This book is dedicated to my family: Robert J., Carol Anne and Carol Marie, the Friels, for their love and support and to Donna, a pretty persuaded.

INTRODUCTION

The ocean is a living and breathing organism. It is a living soup, chunky style, that contains everything from bacteria to Blue Whales. Nowhere in the world is this more evident than in The Bahamas. In this book, I've tried to document some of this life with photographs and write a bit about what I've seen.

I've been diving in The Bahamas many times over the past 10 years but I never stop being impressed by the beauty and sheer quantity of life on these reefs. If you dive, snorkel or sit in a glass bottom boat you know what I mean: Underwater Bahamas is a riot of life.

I hope this book does some justice to my subject. I hope it may impart some information on the coral reef or some appreciation of its splendor. Most of all I hope you enjoy it.

Bob Friel

WEST PALM BEACHS
MIAMI BEACH
West End
GRAND BAHAMA
Walker's Cay
BIMINI
Cat Cay
Freeport Lucaya
CAY SAL
Green Turtle Cay
Treasure Cay
Great Harbour Cay
Marsh Harbour
Hope Town
Chub Cay
BERRY ISLANDS
ABACO
Fresh Creek
ANDROS
NASSAU
Spanish Wells
Cargill Creek
Harbour Island
ELEUTHERA
CAT ISLAND
EXUMA
SAN SALVADOR
RAGGED ISLANDS
Stella Maris
LONG ISLAND
CROOKED ISLAND
ACKLINS
N
MAYAGUANA
GREAT INAGUA
LITTLE INAGUA

THE BAHAMAS BORN OF THE SEA

The Commonwealth of The Bahamas is a land made up of mainly water. The 700 islands, collectively called an archipeligo, are spread thinly over some 100,000 square miles of the Atlantic Ocean. It is a country whose very existence is owed to the ocean and one that is continually built by a living sea.

It was a Bahamian island that was the first land sighted on Columbus's ocean blue in '92 transatlantic tour. This makes The Bahamas the oldest of the New World. When Columbus landed he was greeted by the Lucayans. The Lucayans were the first settlers of The Bahamas. They were a gentle, peaceful people and so were quickly exterminated by the Spanish. The rest of Bahamian history is resplendent with conquistadors and kings, planters and slaves, ship-wrecks and the shipwrecked, rum runners, privateers and pirates.

Tourism has been The Bahamas biggest industry since World War II and, aside from the casino vampires, its visitors have been lured from around the world by its natural beauty. The powdery pink and white beaches, swaying palms and pastel architecture are all here as are picture perfect spots on each island to watch the sun splashdown into a warm sea.

As colorful and exciting as The Bahamas are above the waterline, the islands can be considered subtropical icebergs with at least 90 percent of their attractions found below the surface. While animal life above the waterline is limited mainly to birds and lizards, beneath the surface lies one of the world's richest ecosystems. Bahamian reefs are crowded wall to wall with samples from more plant and animal groups than can be found anywhere on land. And where the Bahama islands are low and relatively featureless above the waterline, few realize that just below the surface are canyons deeper and steeper than those anywhere else on earth. One subsea canyon known as the Providence Channel is 13 thousand feet deep and makes Arizona's Grand Canyon look like a crack in the sidewalk.

If you could see the entire archipeligo without the ocean you'd see that the islands of The Bahamas are actually little, palm-infested bumps on the top of a great limestone plateau built up from the

7

ocean floor. It is a gigantic rock, produced by the sea and covered with only the thinnest veneer of life.

150 million years ago, while dinosaurs were stomping the terra of North America, marine sediments began accumulating in a warm shallow sea. Ocean covered what is now Florida, The Bahamas and most of Cuba. The sediments came from the seawater itself as it was heated by the sun over the shallows. Corals began to colonize and build reefs around these banks of sediment and a circle of life was created. The tiny corals built solid limestone barriers which acted as retaining walls. The sediment behind the reefs was protected from the ocean currents and allowed to sit until it too solidified into limestone. As this limestone bank grew, it weighed down on the earth's crust. The crust sank. The coral growth and sediment process continued for millions of years and the great plateau rose. Around 80 million years ago, currents and erosion split and shaped the plateau and separated The Bahamas from Florida and Cuba. Sea level rose and fell over the geological time, building up islands and allowing the creation of the cuts and passes that have since grown into the deep canyons and channels of the archipeligo.

Still the coral grew like a fortress wall around the edge of the Bahama plateau and still the sediments piled up behind the reef. These sediment banks are what gave the country its name: "Bajio Mar" or shallow sea. The sea is shallow over the banks only because the plateau has been able to grow 20,000 feet high off the sea floor at a fraction of an inch at a time.

Today these processes continue just as they did 150 million years ago. There are a lot fewer dinosaurs in North America now but the corals and marine sediments ceaselessly build towards the sun and continue to create The Bahamas.

GREAT CIRCLE OF LIFE

The coral reef is the most amazing ecosystem on earth. It grows, thrives and creates its own environment while surrounded by ocean waters that are relatively devoid of everything needed to support life. It is an oasis in a desert of water water everywhere.

The coral reef supports an unparalleled diversity of life. Yes, I know that at present count the rainforest supports more species, but let's face it, most of them are bugs. When you move above the classifications of species and genus, the reef is more diverse. The coral reefs are also the most massive structures ever built by living things. The entire Bahama Plateau: 500 miles long and 200 miles wide, exists only because tiny animals and plants were able to build its 20,000 foot high walls.

The incredible profusion of life on the reef and its great building achievements are only possible through the tightest recycling of the materials of life among its creatures and the reef structure itself. The plants and animals have evolved together to form a completely interlocking system of relationships that form a great circle of life.

People were confused about coral for a long time. They didn't know wether coral was a plant, animal or just a nice shade of pink. They were first described as plants because of their appearance and need for sunlight but corals are actually animals with internal vegetables that produce minerals. The corals that build the reefs of The Bahamas are closely related to the jellyfish and anemones. They are a group of 'gummy' animals with simple, jelly-filled bodies and complex lives.

Reef-building corals are colonial with each individual unit called a polyp. The polyps are tiny yet form the building blocks of the world's great reefs. Each polyp secretes a limestone structure in which it lives. The polyp then has the ability to clone itself and create a colony of polyps which all build their own stone fortresses and thus slowly build up the reef. Each polyp in the colony shares tissue with the others and, if you allow that there is a continuity of life beginning with that first polyp and extending through possibly a million clones, the largest coral heads you see in Bahamas are animals hundreds of years old and may be the longest lived creatures on earth.

Corals can only build reefs on the right substrate in clear, warm water where there is little suspended sediment and just the right salinity. They need clear water and only grow down to about 100 feet because they must capture the sun's energy. Every food chain, except the deep sea vents, is driven by photosynthesis. Somewhere there has to be plants capable of converting the sun's radiation into usable organic compounds. On the reef the most important plants are contained within the very tissues of the coral animal itself. This relationship, beneficial to both plant and animal and necessary for the very existence of the reef, is called a symbiosis.

The symbiotic plants are an algae that live in all species of coral that are able to build reefs. In fact, the algae are a necessity if the corals are to build large structures. The relationship is a model of recycling. The algae uses the coral's waste products as fertilizer. The carbon dioxide exhaled by the polyp is fixed into carbohydrates by the plant and then leaked back to the coral as food. Another by-product of photosynthesis is oxygen which the polyp needs to breathe. The presence of the algae also induces the coral to lay down its skeleton at a much faster rate and thus directly helps to build the reef structure upon which each of the innumerable species of plants and animals depend for life.

There are millions of these single-cell plants per square inch of coral tissue. The algae are brown and give color to the otherwise transparent polyps. When placed under stress, the coral expels much of the algae from its gut and takes on the white color of its limestone skeleton. This phenomenon is known as bleaching and has occurred in corals all over The Bahamas twice in the past 10 years. The stress was caused by the water temperatures rising above what the corals find tolerable.

A great concern is that global warming and ozone depletion will raise the average sea temperature a few degrees and expose the earth to increased UV radiation more quickly then the corals can adapt and evolve to the new conditions. If this happens, the corals will be killed by diseases which grow better in warmer water or overgrown by organisms which can survive the stress more successfully. Whatever happens, the corals will die and the reefs will cease to grow. The circle of life will be broken.

The reef is often called a fragile ecosystem. It is not. It is a hardy system that has used its slow and steady growth as a defense against the ravages of hurricanes, plagues and changes in the environment through the millennia. Unfortunately, the reef, like every other ecosystem, is facing changes that are happening at a faster pace then ever

Each coral polyp builds a limestone cup.

The polyp emerges at night to feed on plankt...

Each polyp in the same colony is a clone.

Brain coral polyps share a body wall but each have individual mouths

before in the history of life on earth. Man's manipulation of the world's environment is a severe test of every other species' evolvability, and corals may not be up to it. One organism that can thrive in higher water temperatures and increased incidence of UV light is fire coral. These stinging hydroids may be able to completely out-compete the weakened corals and overgrow entire reefs. And you thought there was too much fire coral on the reef already.

Corals grow in many different shapes even within the same species. Their structures are adapted to maximize exposure to the sun and minimize the damage from wave and storm energy. In protected, well-lit areas, the corals grow into intricate shapes. In high energy places where they are exposed to strong surge, they tend to grow massive, stable skeletons. In deeper water, the corals must grow in shapes that allow their symbiotic algae the best chance to capture the sun's energy. Deep water reef-building corals are most often in flattened, plate-like forms.

Along with cloning, corals can reproduce by fragmentation. Staghorn corals use the destructive power of storms to their benefit. When pieces of the brittle colony are broken off, the fragments can settle and begin to clone themselves into new colonies. Vast forests of staghorn may be born of just one individual polyp that cloned and spread by being broken and scattered.

The problem with these forms of asexual reproduction is that they produce simple copies of the 'parent' animal. There is no mixing of genes. If the parent is genetically vulnerable to a specific stress then the entire colony will be vulnerable. To allow for genetic mixing, which keeps evolution alive and well, the corals also reproduce sexually. This makes for a stronger, more resilient population and helps to ensure that entire species cannot be wiped out by a single event. The corals produce a free swimming larvae that attempts to settle on a suitable substrate and then immediately begins to secrete its limestone skeleton and grow into a colony.

Space is at a premium on the reefs of the Bahamas and corals must compete with sponges, forams, hydroids, anemones, algae and other corals for prime real estate. The competition is fierce and each group has developed weapons and strategies to limit or kill the others. Corals have tentacles armed with stinging cells just like their cousins the jellyfish. They use these to defend themselves as well as to capture tiny animals to put a little meat in their diet.

Coral needs the   symbiotic algae

Corals under stress are prone to disease...

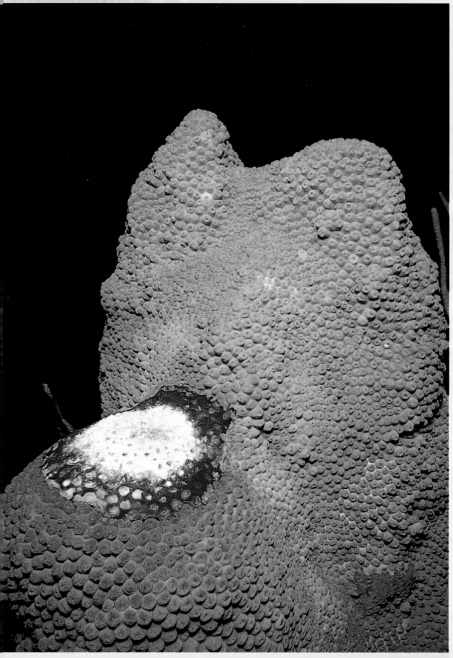

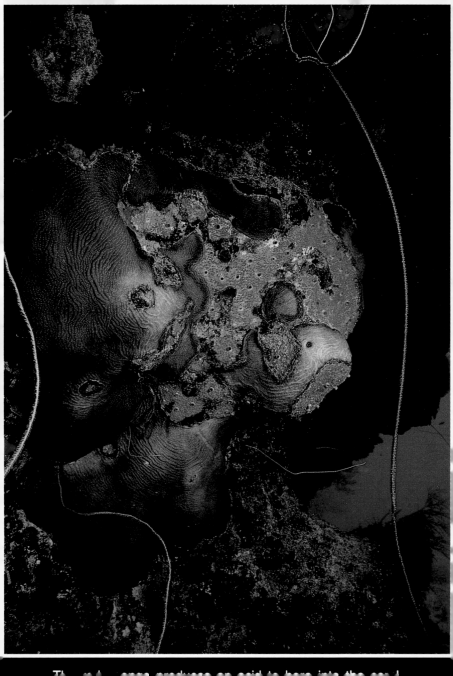

The sea urchin produces an acid to bore into the coral.

The Orange Ball Corallimorpharian
is in the same class of animals as corals and anemones

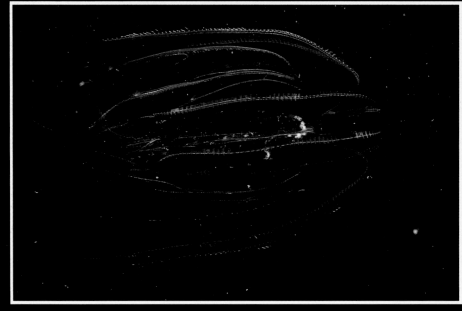

Comb Jelly

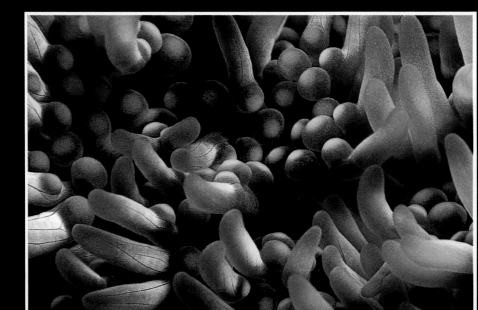

Sponges are the most primitive animals on the reef

Sponges of form

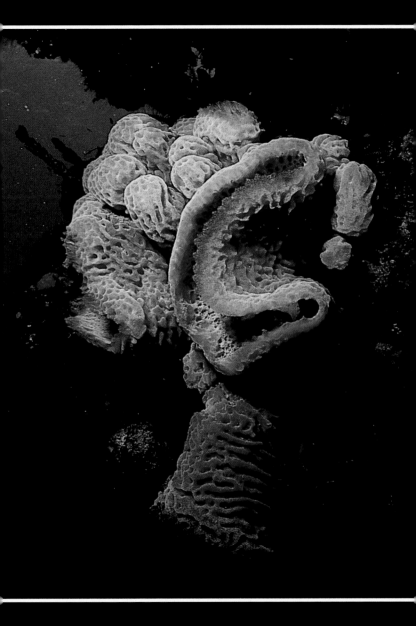

Sponges filter food from currents that run through their bodies.

Sponges of every conceivable shape and color live on the Bahama reefs

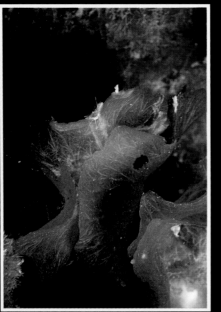

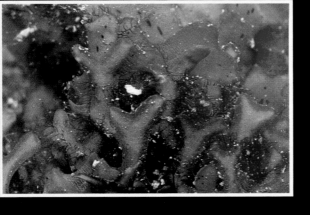

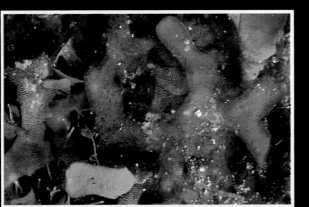

Red Night Shrimp

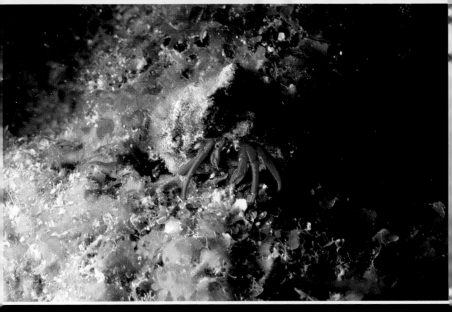

Red Reef Hermit

Hairy Crab

Decorator crabs cover their shells with reef growth as a camouflage.

A tiny crab hid _____ of a brain coral.

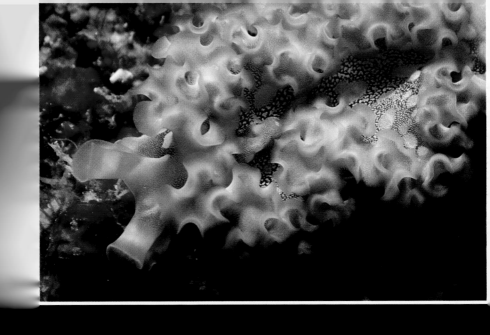

Flamingo Tongue Snail   feeds on a sea fan's polyps.

Rough Fileclam

Long-horned Nudibranch

Conch: mollusc

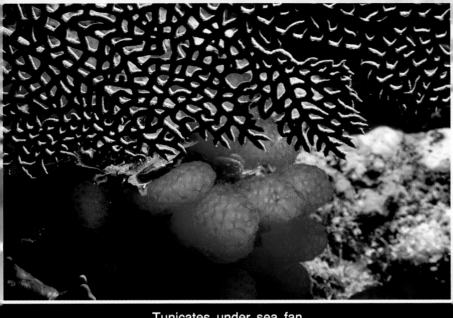

Tunicates under sea fan

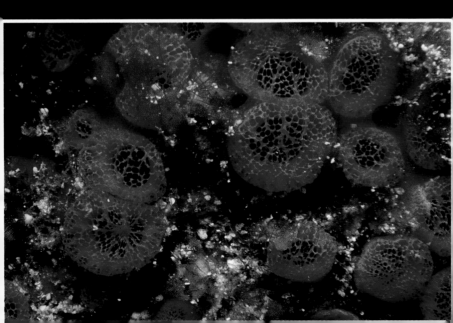

Painted Tunicates

Reef urchin

Brittle Starfish laying eggs

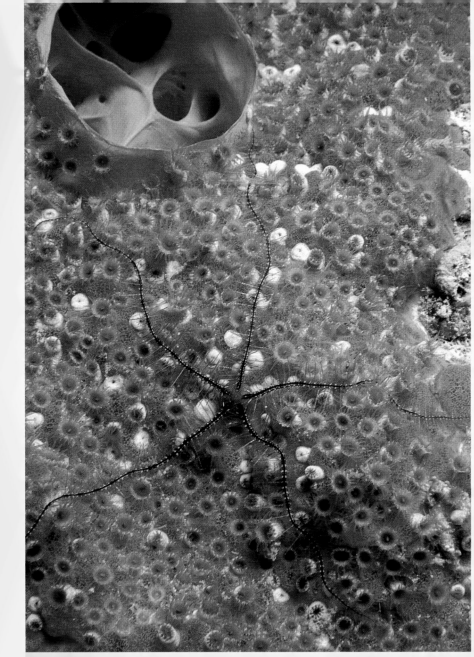

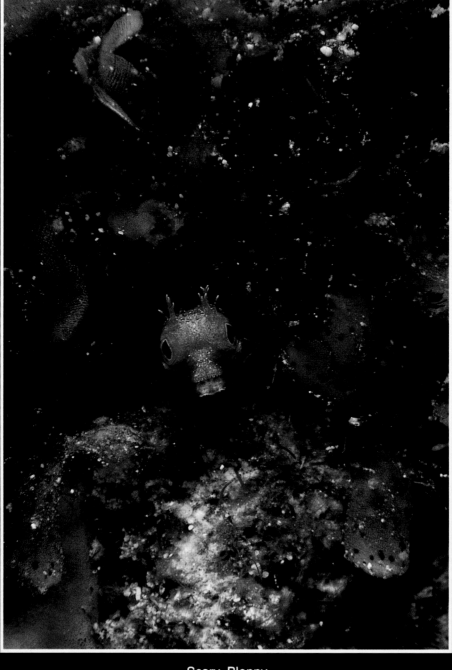

Scary Blenny

A tiny Triplefin hides among the polyps of a Brain Coral.

Triplefin

Fairy Basslet

Trumpetfish are ...he Bahama reef,

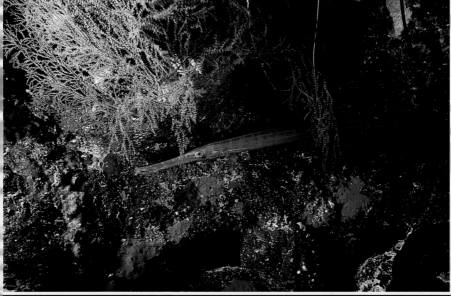

Trumpetfish use camouflage and lightning fast stabs to catch small fish

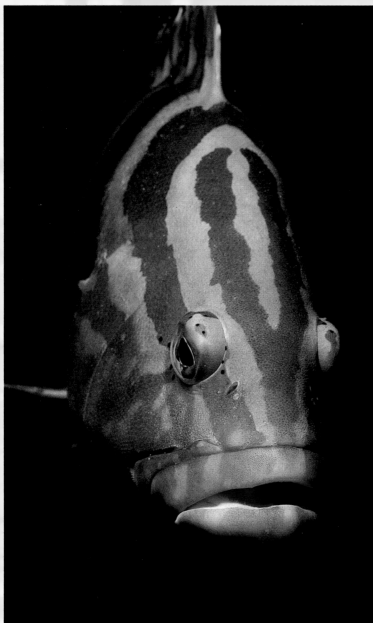

Nassau Groupers are the master gulpers of the Bahama reef

Barracuda

The Cuda is another stalking predator.

Sand Diver

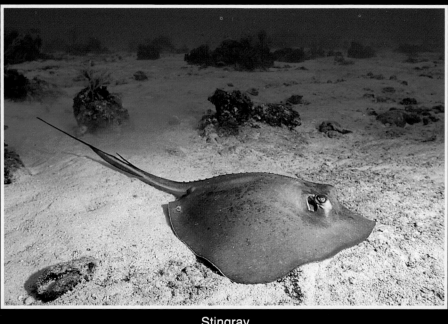

Stingray
These are ambush predators.

Scorpionfish

They use camouflage to make them invisible to prey.

Puffer

Parrot

Hamlet

Queen Trigger

French Angels

Loggerhead
Turtles are common on Bahama reefs.

Barred Hamlet

Blueheaded Wrasse dance.

RELATIONSHIPS

There are many other examples of symbiosis between the reefs inhabitants besides the coral-algae cooperation. These symbiosis illustrate the long evolution and high degree of interconnectedness in the coral world of The Bahamas.

Cleaning stations are the most visible of the symbiotic relationships and are the most fun to look for underwater. The stations are usually on some prominent reef feature such as a coral head surrounded by sand. The cleaners are small fish and shrimp that survive by eating the dead skin and parasites off of larger creatures. The cleaners are brightly colored to attract attention. Their colors and activities also give them some protection from the reef's predators who respect the importance of the cleaners as healers. This is not a blanket policy however, and cleaning animals have been found in quite a few stomachs of Bahamian fish and eels.

The cleaner fish dance and the shrimp wave their extra-long antennas to signal they are open for business. Fish that want to be cleaned will gather around or line up and hold themselves still. The cleaners go over their entire bodies and the fish, even barracuda, patiently open their mouths and gill covers to allow the cleaners access.

Divers can gently approach these stations and watch the process. Shrimp will sometimes jump onto an extended hand and run around picking at your fingernails. If this happens, remember to place the shrimp back where it came from. A small shrimp left floating in the water column or scrambling across the sand will quickly become seafood.

Other relationships have developed between shrimp, crabs and anemones where the crustaceans find protection within the poisonous stinging cells of the anemone's tentacles. It is not certain what service, if any, the shrimp and crabs perform for their hosts. There are other, parasitic, relationships common to the reef. Small bug-like isopods attach to soldier fish and butterfly fish and feed off their hosts. Remoras, or shark-suckers, stick on to sharks, rays and turtles and hitch free rides. They serve no benefit to the larger animals and can only make life more difficult for them by producing drag.

The Spotted Cleaner Shrimp...

and Banded Clinging Crab often live in association with the Giant Anemone

Remoras also catch rides on smaller fish such as this parrotfish.

This isoped   Soldierfish

Small fish find protection among the stinging cells of fire coral.

Creole Wrasse

The Blue Tang use schooling to help them feed.

Boga use schooling to help them not <u>become</u> feed.

Dayschool of grunts and soldierfish

Find the diver

Silversides

Barjack hunt in packs.

Barjack herding Silversides

CLOSE ENCOUNTERS

Several dive operators in The Bahamas now run special programs that allow their guests the chance to spend time in the water with dolphins, whales and sharks.

It is possible to see these animals on other 'regular' dives but it is not likely. I had extraordinary luck in just the few weeks prior to the completion of this book and swam with wild dolphins, Pilot Whales and several wild sharks on trips planned just to dive on reefs. This was unusual luck, especially for me. There are, however, a few ways to better your chances of getting close to these animals: you can go out and find them, go down and attract them or catch them and train them. There are operators using each of these methods in The Bahamas.

Several live-aboard boats run trips that take divers and snorkelers out to meet wild dolphins. The animals give no guarantee that they'll show up and some groups of divers have had hours of swimming and playing with large dolphin families while others have spent days getting only brief looks at transient animals.

If you do get a chance to swim with wild dolphins you will immediately forgive any hours spent bobbing around the bank waiting for them. You'll get to see them interact naturally with each other and with their environment. You'll hear the clicks and whistles as they communicate and search for food in the sandy bottom. You'll see beauty, strength and personality. The dolphin will often approach very close and seem to really enjoy watching our feeble attempts at imitating their graceful "dolphin kick." They will actually make fun us divers by coming alongside and doing their own jerky imitations of our swimming ability.

The best of the wild dolphin trips will be led by a marine life naturalist who can answer your questions and make the experience better for the diver and safer for the dolphins.

A couple of dive operators are attempting similar wild experiences with another marine mammal, the Pilot Whale. The whales spend a part of their year in the Tongue of The Ocean between Nassau and Andros. While I was researching this book, I encountered the whales on my way out to photograph Silky Sharks with Nassau's Stuart Cove. The whales were in large pods and we first mistook them for dolphin. A second look and we could tell they were much larger animals. As our dive boat approached closer we fully expected them to sound. They didn't. I got into the water as quickly as possible and was able to spend about 10 minutes, a true "moment", with one of these little whales.

It was a beautiful animal, about 18 feet long, with a stubby tail. The whale was obviously aware of my presence but it did not move away. It kept its course and its leisurely pace as it swam just below the surface. It rose about every 6 kicks and grabbed a breath of the same air I was breathing through my snorkel. As I watched the afternoon sun dance patterns across the whale's back I began to regret not having a camera ready before jumping in the water. But, when the whale looked me over and we seemed, for a moment, to make eye contact, I was happy not to have been looking through the small frame of a viewfinder.

Just as with the wild dolphins, an encounter with free swimming whales will be a once in a lifetime event for most people. If trips can be successfully run to see the Pilot Whales they will be well worth the effort.

Another type of experience has been pioneered at UNEXSO in Freeport. It is a captive release program using Atlantic Bottlenose Dolphins. Captive release means you are not put into a closed pen with the dolphins but that the dolphins are trained to swim out and join you on an open water reef. I am not really an advocate of any captive program: I once freed a pheasant under glass, but I strongly believe in the value of education and interactive experience. These captive dolphins aren't made to jump through hoops or ring bells. Their "tricks" are to let divers touch their skin, feel their teeth and hear their voices. They have been trained more for education than entertainment. They are not forced to interact with people and I have been there when they've refused. Once out of their home lagoon, the dolphins don't have to return. They could simply swim away but so far they haven't. They live in a large facility, are served their meals and are protected from sharks. They may always come back just because life is so much easier for them in captivity.

it if necessary. The sharks key on the bait. They can smell and taste it from far away and it turns them on immediately. When the stimulus is removed, the sharks will settle down just as quickly.

Dives where the scent is controlled and the food portioned out slowly are the best for photography and overall viewing. The so-called "frenzy" dives where a large amount of bait is released into the water at one time are the least safe and also the worst for watching the sharks.

As for the safety of the person feeding the shark? I'm reminded of something my Dad told me when I got my first pocket knife. "Son," he addressed me, "you now have a knife and you've got to accept that you're gonna get cut." I remember pondering this for quite awhile before sinking the blade deep into his leg.

Feed sharks long enough and one will accidentally nip you. Feed sharks wrong enough and you better be carrying a staple gun and a lot of insurance.

Several shark species are indigenous to The Bahamas. Lemon sharks, Bull Sharks, Tigers and Hammerheads are all occasionally seen patrolling the reefs of The Bahamas. Oceanic Whitetips and Mako Sharks have been reported from the Tongue of The Ocean while there have been even rarer sightings of Whale Sharks in the offshore surface waters of the archipeligo.

The sharks that dive operators have been able to draw in and feed consistently are the Caribbean Reef, Silky, Sharpnose and Nurse Sharks. Reef Sharks are often mistaken for Bull Sharks so it is not certain wether the Bulls are taking advantage of the handouts. But there have been no Bulls at the feedings I've witnessed.

Sharpnose Shark

Nurse Shark

A young Caribbean Reef Shark

The Silky

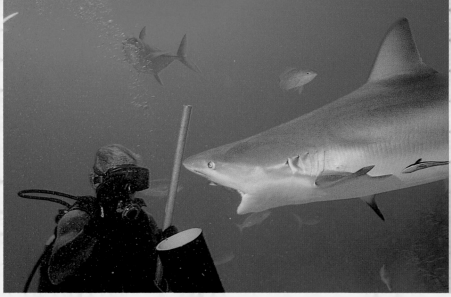

Yes I is a carnivore... that is what these teeth is for!

'Sea itch' has become a generic name for the results of stings and things from a variety of invertebrates. There is a more common term used for it: "Sea Lice," but that brings to mind a group of hairy sea monkeys sitting around grooming each other and I can't quite deal with that. Sea Itch is most common in the warmer months in The Bahamas, the summer season, especially in stirred up water. The itchy welts are caused by a few different organisms with the most common being a drifting phase of a type of sea anemone and another the marine phase of a parasite that works its way from fish to birds. The most effective way of avoiding sea itch seems to be stripping and thoroughly rinsing yourself off as soon after getting out of the water as possible. If you have visible stings, or if you feel burning, then use vinegar first before fresh water.

Some people are more susceptible to sea stings than others just as they are to bees. A couple of species such as the Portuguese Man of War and the Sea Wasp can cause trouble no matter how susceptible you are. Any serious symptoms like difficulty breathing should of course be treated by a doctor.

STICKERS

Stickers are those fish and invertebrates that use spines as defense. There are no animals in The Bahamas that can shoot or throw spines at you. You must go to them and step or sit on them in order to be injured.

The sea urchin is another master protector of the reef. After a diver has spent time picking urchin spines out of his assaulted flesh, he will long remember to stay neutrally buoyant and not lay on the reef. The urchins are nocturnal grazers and the best chance to see them is at night when they are out of their holes. The most threatening of the urchin species in The Bahamas is the diadema, or long-spined sea urchin. Its brittle spines can be up to 18 inches long and are barbed in such a way that when they go in they don't want to come out without a fight. In the 1980's a water borne pathogen spread around the Caribbean, Florida and The Bahamas that killed off almost the entire long-spined urchin population. It was news as good for careless night divers as it was bad for the reef's ecosystem. The diadema have started to come back strong in some areas while they are still absent in others. If you land afoul of a sea urchin get as much of the spine out as possible without causing more damage than the original injury. It is better to leave small bits of the spine to dissolve under your skin than to try major surgery with dive knives and dull spoons.

Fire worms are beautiful animals that feed on corals and anemones. The worms have a furry-looking border made up of thousands of tiny bristles that can break off into the skin and burn like all get out.

Stingrays and Scorpionfish are predators adapted to hiding on the bottom in ambush. You'll find that most animals that spend their lives sitting around in an environment where things are constantly trying to eat each other will have evolved some kind of defense. Stingrays and Scorpionfish use spines to keep the bigger fish off their backs and divers are simply the clumsiest, loudest and ugliest of the big fish. As threatening as the big spines on stingrays look, I have never heard of anyone swimming or diving that was hit by one. It is mainly a danger to people wading in the shallows, although simply shuffling your feet will send the rays flapping away. The Scorpionfish has a set of big, thick spines arrayed on its dorsal surface: its back. Again, I have not known anyone hurt by one of these passive, gargoyle-like fish. They are so sure of their camouflage that experienced and careful divers can lift them up off the reef by moving very slowly and gently.

BITERS

I once knew a divemaster whose one finger was shorter than it should have been. Its tip had been bitten cleanly off by a fish. It wasn't a shark. It wasn't a 'cuda. It wasn't even a razor-toothed blenny. Embarrassingly for the divemaster, his finger was lost to the dreaded pufferfish. He had chased down and caught a large puffer and was showing his enthralled dive group how the fish sucks in water and blows itself up like a balloon when threatened. He was not paying very close attention because, after all, puffers are slow, passive and they dress funny. The divemaster let his finger come around to the front of the fish where the fused teeth of its `beak' are conveniently located and the fish simply did what was natural. Again it shows that nothing is out to get you but that every animal will defend itself when molested. Harassment accounts for the few bites caused by Nurse Sharks and any fish you can grab at like the puffers. Most other fish won't let you get close enough to touch them.

142

Barracuda are the mayors of the Bahamian reefs. They have to know everything that's going on. They will congregate under boats at anchor and will approach divers and sometimes follow them around for an entire dive. They are sleek, fierce-looking fish. Their mouths are usually open at least enough to allow you to see the sharp spikes they use for teeth. A barracuda attacking a prey fish is a humbling sight. The cuda often hunts just below the surface, using its predator's eye to scan the fish below and taking advantage of its countershaded body, invisible against the bright surface. When it sees a likely prey, the fish acts instantly. Its long, muscular body can fly as straight and fast as an arrow at the prey. If you are lucky enough to be close to the attack you will see all the fish in the area counting their fins and tails to see if they were the ones hit. The attack is that fast. The cuda will take an entire fish if it fits into its mouth or can just as easily cut it cleanly in two and then turn back to swallow the other half.

Barracuda do look nasty. Their image problem is not helped by their ready smile. Also their habit of following divers around is sometimes genuinely unnerving. But they will not attack a human in clear water and, for the record: The waters of The Bahamas are very clear. Their feeding instinct can be triggered by the flash of any shiny object. They may move in even closer to examine a reflective watch or other mirror-like surfaces but Barracuda have excellent eyesight and if they can see that the object is attached to you they will not make a go for it. If at any time a Barracuda is showing more than just an intense curiosity in you and seems aggressive, the chances are that it is used to being fed by divers. These fish sometimes have to be shooed away by swimming directly at them or waving a fin in their face. This brings up the real chance of being bit by a fish.

The great majority of people who are bled by marine fishes are holding food at the time. There seems to be some confusion out there as to the term "hand-feeding." Think of how many people are bit when they feed strange domestic animals or even their own pets. The reef fish are not pets, they are wild animals. We like to think of the reef as a soothing, calm place and it is for us but, for the animals living there, it is a world where they must kill, eat and run or else they get killed, eaten and miss the prom.

Yellowtail Snappers, Sergeant Majors and Bermuda Chub will swarm around divers on those Bahamian reefs where they have been fed. They will tug at your hair and nip at your ears to get your attention. The Yellowtails and Sergeant majors will sometimes draw blood and can be as maddening as 2 pound mosquitoes.

The real danger in feeding the schooling fish is that something bigger might want some. Barracuda, groupers and moray eels attack their food very quickly and very seriously. If you must feed the smaller fish, do not hold the bait in your hand. Carry the food in a re-sealable container that prevents the scent from escaping and use it to shake the food into the water. Keep a lookout at all times for any of the secondary predators that might have been attracted and seal up the bait quickly if they approach. The small reef fish often become so competitive with each other for the free handouts that they themselves forget to watch for predators and it is not uncommon at all for a cuda to hang around and chew up a few of the cute little fish that the divers have been feeding.

I don't recommend that any pleasure diver even attempt to feed the bigger fish and eels. The divers you see pictured in magazines have usually worked for years to gain the experience and always have the scars to prove it.

The reality and perception of the dangers lurking in Underwater Bahamas are very different. The perception that something big and toothy will maliciously attack is wrong. The real danger, as usual, is man himself. We can indeed be injured by marine life but it is through our own carelessness and callousness that leads us to come into contact with animals that must protect themselves. The 2 golden rules of diving should be: Don't Hold Your Breath and Stay Off the Reef. Actually the most common and the worst injury that divers and snorkelers receive, aside from having their skulls gnawed by giant squid, are simple cuts from any surface of the reef. Bacteria play a major role in the sea and life on the reef would not exist at all if not for their ability to efficiently decompose organic matter. Every surface is covered with bacteria and a cut can stay infected for a long time or even go septic if not treated properly. First aid for minor cuts includes a cleaning with hydrogen peroxide and then exposing the wound to the air to kill off any anaerobic bacteria present before applying a topical antibiotic. Cuts can be prevented simply by staying neutrally buoyant and keeping off the reef.

By taking care not to hurt the reef environment you will be taking care of yourself. And the only thing really waiting for you underwater in The Bahamas is a wonderful experience.

Moray Eel

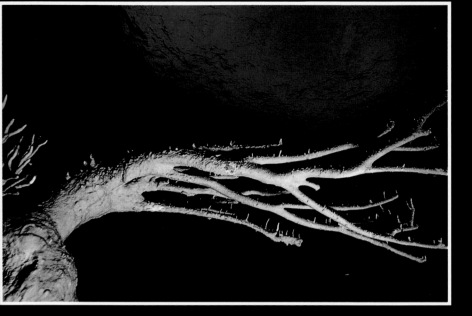

Fire Coral

The stinging cells are visible in a close-up of Fire Coral

The Edge

Astronauts step out of their capsules and into space. They float weightless while their world spins below and the stars shine above.

It must be a truly wondrous experience but I don't think it can compete with diving on a wall...

As a diver, you can swim along a living coral spur as clouds of brightly colored fish pulse and pour among the soft corals. Suddenly in front of you there is Blue. You swim a bit further and the reef drops away. You've flown off the edge of the world. Here you hang weightless. The Blue in front of you becomes deeper as you look down. The color reaches into you and pulls your eyes further and further down. Above you, the sun is a burst of rays and an aquamarine splash that quickly melts into deeper blues. You are in space. But it is not the cold, sterile vacuum of outer space. It is a space filled with living creatures and the ethereal wakes of creatures past.

Life was born in the sea. Some forms dragged themselves up onto land. A few of the most highly evolved beasts have since returned to the sea and when I float out over a coral wall I think I know why.

Black Coral

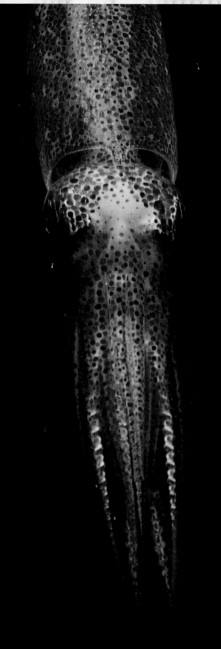

Dusk To Dawn
The Magic Hours

Some of the most amazing dives I've ever done have been when I slipped into the water while the sun was still about a finger's width above the horizon and then just floated above the reef. This is the most exciting time to be underwater in The Bahamas.

Predators move quickly over the reef. They do not swim with the unhurried grace that marks their daytime patrols. Now they are on the hunt. The other fish know it and there is an electricity all over the reef like among the savannah beasts when the lions are up and about.

The predators work best in this confused light. The day-time fish rush about trying to find safe harbor for the night but their eyes start to fail as the sun falls. The nocturnal fish start to appear but they too are not adapted to see best at this time and are vulnerable.

The large schools of grunts that spend the day drifting in the shade of elkhorn branches now gather up and proceed in a line to the back reef where they spend the night feeding on shrimp among the grass beds.

You can look up and watch the purple of the night slowly swallow the aquamarine surface of the day. For a moment everything is quiet. A school of jacks rush by at full speed and then all is still again. The reef looks barren. Then there is almost imperceptible movement. Crinoids crawl out of their holes and spider-walk up the reef. Basket stars carefully untangle their intricate arms and spread them into the current. The hard stone of the reef corals softens as you see each polyp extend its translucent tentacles. Tiny cardinal fish and squirrel fish are suddenly all over the reef. Sea urchins move out over the sand and moray eels snake among the coral heads and slide in and out of holes hoping to bump into sleeping fish. A Parrotfish brazenly sleeps in the open but when you move closer you see that it has built itself a sleeping bag made of bubbles to hide its scent.

Once it is darker you can switch on your light. The reef now bursts into color wherever you aim your torch. Brilliant red eyes of shrimp glow everywhere. A movement catches your eye. An octopus flows along the reef. It melts into an impossibly small hole when you approach but it quickly brings its head back out to take a look. If you extend a hand the octopus will reach out a suckered arm and curiously feel your skin. A crab leaves cover for a moment and the octopus is on it immediately. Turn your light back off. When your eyes adjust, you notice living light everywhere around you. Wave your hand near a sponge covered with brittle stars and bolts of blue fire run up and down their arms. Large fish that swim by you leave glowing wakes to mark their paths. Run your hand through the water and you too control the stars.

My tanks never hold enough air for dives during the magic

Octopus
Nocturnal Hunter

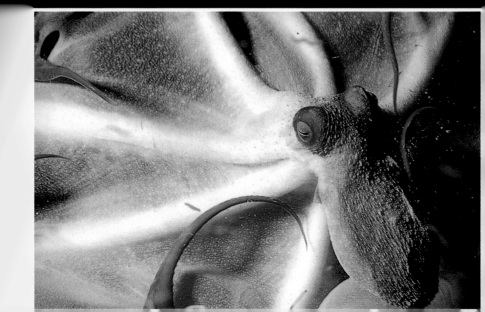

Stinging cells appear as white dots covering coral's tentacles.

Corals become carnivores at night fall.

BLUE HOLES

Imagine a native Lucayan fisherman of long ago crossing the flats in a small skiff. Suddenly he sees a dark blue stain in the water come alive. It begins to swirl faster and faster until it becomes a whirlpool. Another time and another tide the water boils up with clouds of white fluff spewed from this bowel of the earth. If the fisherman dropped his anchor or fishing line in the dark patch it could fall hundreds of feet and not hit bottom. If he put a bait out to catch one of the small jacks he saw enter the hole, there might be a sudden great tug and the line would be bitten in two.

Experiences like these with blue holes might not have been enough to make the fisherman give up the sea and turn to farming but I'm sure they'd make some great campfire stories. The wonderful thing about The Bahamas' blue holes is that the stories are still true today. They are mysterious places where great forces battle and sea monsters dwell.

The blue holes may not be bottomless but the deepest are over 350 feet and that is conventionally bottomless for divers and snorkelers. The Bahamas contain the only known "tidal" blue holes. These are effected by the ocean tides that suck water in and blow it back out the holes. This causes the water above shallow holes to swirl like a drain or conversely to fill the water column with a bizarre, fluffy algae that make it look like a giant cotton candy machine.

And yes there are sea monsters in Bahama blue holes. On Andros there is a blind, full-grown barracuda in a hole that appears to be completely landlocked. On the Cay Sal Bank there is a blue hole filled with sharks and King Mackerel big enough to eat the sharks. Another Cay Sal hole may be the lost secret burial ground of the conchs.

Most of the blue holes in the Bahamas are shallow, bowl-shaped pits that are filled with sand and the shells of gastropods that just couldn't help trying to peek over the rim. Other holes, especially those with water flowing through them, have remained open and free of sediment.

The deepest blue hole has been measured at 363 feet. There was one hole where a plumb line never touched bottom but it is believed that the line shot out a hole and went down over the wall.

The holes are named because, from above, the deeper water is much bluer than the surrounding shallows. The holes were created by water but not, as you might think, by the eroding action of seawater. The blue holes and the extensive cave systems that honeycomb The Bahama islands were all created above sea level by fresh water. Even before the industrial revolution, rain water has been slightly acidic. Over recent geological time the sea level has gone up and down some 400 feet. When the sea was at its lowest, The Bahama Plateau was a great towering mass that rose out of the water. Rain water pooled and ran across the limestone and slowly melted through the rock. It can be proven that the caves and blue holes were born in the air by the evidence of dripstones: stalactites and stalagmites, and the beautiful patterns called drip curtains deep down inside the limestone structure. The only time these features can form is when fresh water seeps through limestone, picks up a load of calcium and drips it into a cave. The dissolved minerals solidify in the air and form stony icicles.

Diving in the blue holes is wonderful. The visibility is often poor but that makes it even more exciting. Many of the holes were once giant caverns whose roofs fell in. When you descend the walls you often find them slanting past the vertical.

Some of the holes have caves leading off the main chambers. The bottoms of the caves are often covered with fine sediment that reduces visibility to zero once you kick just a few feet inside. No one should venture into these without the proper training, equipment and an experienced guide.

UNDERWATER BAHAMAS TOUR

This section is a tour of the diving available throughout The Bahamas. There is an infinite number of dive "spots" possible in the island group so wherever possible, I've kept from naming specific dives. I'll just try to describe the major features of each area and leave the naming up to the local professionals. A problem with naming spots is that every diver who reads a dive "guide" goes to whatever island and feels cheated if he or she doesn't get to go on the dives written about. The operators then have to schedule those dives all the time and can get lazy and not fulfill their responsibility of finding new dives. Every dive guide will be subjective unless it lists every single dive in the country. As this book is not anything like most guides, I'm not even going to try. Plus I don't want the responsibility of writing that "Curly's Reef" is the best dive off of "Stooge's Cay." I'd have some of you sending me nasty letters, scrawled in crayon, telling me you had a lousy dive there and that "Shemp's Cave" is so much better and I don't know a good dive from a septic tank. So this will give you a good idea of the reef structure and types of diving available in each group of islands in The Bahamas. I've always found that local guides are by far the best way to get to the best spots once you're in the area. I have not had a "bad" dive anywhere in The Bahamas and I've found something of interest to photograph every time I've been underwater here. You can take it for granted that on any island where there are dive support facilities there will be dives you will enjoy if you swim slow and keep your eyes open.

BIMINI

The Biminis are a group of small islands that perch on the western edge of what we've called the Bahama Plateau. The Gulf Stream has shaped this side of the archipeligo and was the force that originally split the primordial Bahamas from South Florida 80 million years ago.

The "Stream" together with the edge of the plateau combine for exciting drift diving. The edge of the plateau's wall off Bimini is too deep for any serious reef coral growth, but it is lushly covered with soft corals. The Gulf Stream and deep drop off mean that there is the possibility of seeing anything off the wall. Sharks and rays are common while I've also had the rare oppurtunity to see a Blue Marlin off this wall.

Inshore of the wall are deep, medium and shallow reef lines. The deep and medium reefs have large coral heads scattered over sandy bottom while the shallow line is low profile but more continuous. Pelagic fish are common to the deeper reefs with large schools of reef fish inshore. The Gulf Stream seems to make everything grow bigger around Bimini, or maybe it's just the fountain of youth supposedly in the area. I've seen bigger examples of everything from Nurse Sharks to Lettuce Slugs in the waters near these islands.

Twice I've gotten to snorkel with wild dolphins off Bimini. They were chance encounters but are possible at anytime. The (in) famous Bimini Road is in a shallow area off North Bimini. Geologists explain it as a relatively common formation of solidified sand called beach rock. The rock splits into regular shaped blocks that follow the lines of the ancient beach front. Others others have sworn that the long straight line of carved rocks is actually Elvis's secret lunch counter.

Bimini also has a wreck that's great for photos and attracts a lot of pelagic fish. And there is excellent night diving with loads of life in a relatively small, shallow area.

GRAND BAHAMA

If you can drag yourself out of the duty free shops and casinos for a few minutes Grand Bahama has some great diving.

The diving off this large island includes deep, medium and shallow reefs as well as walls, wrecks, wild and captive-release dolphin encounters and shark feeding dives.

Around the Freeport/Lucaya area are several outstanding 'man-made' dives. Theo's Wreck was sent down as a diver's playhouse and sits on the very edge of the wall. It's a good wreck for pictures and fun for a long swim through. The shark-feeding dive off Lucaya is done very well. The sharks are Caribbean Reefs and I've seen up to 12 come in at a time. It's a bit difficult for pictures on account of the fine sand bottom that is easily stirred up but it is still a terrific dive.

UNEXSO's dolphin program that I covered earlier is here at Lucaya as well. You can visit the 9 acre facility to meet the dolphins and then go out to a shallow reef to dive with them.

ABACOS

The Abacos make up the northernmost of the Bahama islands and the best snow skiing in the country is found here.

The general make-up underwater is a fringing reef on the outer slope that encloses a deep lagoon. Most of the dives are within the fringing reef and are relatively shallow. Abaco diving is bottom time diving. The 'old growth' coral inside the lagoon is fantastic. It often grows as a great mass from the sand bottom up until it just barely breaks the surface. These reefs are honeycombed with tunnels and caves, split with crevices and undercut with overhangs that run deep into the structure.

Off Green Turtle Cay there is an area of reef with great canyons and an overhang that goes back at least 80 feet into the reef. The underside is covered with bright yellow cup corals and the cavern fill with silversides.

Inside the lagoon off Marsh Harbour, the masses of coral are hollowed with caves and caverns. One large cavern has a ceiling like a cathedral. Some of the caves run hundreds of feet through the coral and fill with thousands of silversides in the summer.

There are quite a few wrecks off of the Abacos, some dating back to the civil war. One, the San Jacinto, has some nice high profile structure for photos and is home to a curious and large green moray and a couple of Caribbean Reef Sharks.

The Little Bahama Bank, on which the Abacos sit, is another of the places where divers have been able to interact with wild Spotted Dolphins.

NEW PROVIDENCE

New Providence is Nassau's island. It sits on the Lip of the ocean where the Tongue comes out. Nassau is the bright lights and big city of The Bahamas and has the biggest variety of nightlife. If you can get out of bed the next morning, the diving here will open your eyes.

The walls off Nassau have some of the best sponge growth I've seen anywhere. There are also a lot of large features: overhangs and cuts, through the wall that make for great dives. There's a mess of wrecks here as well as a popular blue hole.

Stuart Cove has pioneered a number of shark dives off Nassau and stages encounters with Caribbean Reef Sharks inshore and at the wall as well as with Silky Sharks at the Deer Island Buoy 12 miles into the Tongue of The Ocean.

This is also where we were able to swim with the Pilot Whales in late June.

BERRY ISLANDS

The Berry's, specifically Chub Cay, has miles of excellent walls just like Nassau. This is no surprise since it too sits at the beginning of the Tongue of The Ocean. There is a great mix of fish life here and you may see as many big pelagic species as reef fish.

ANDROS

Andros is the biggest of the Bahama islands. Its west coast is mainly mangroves, mud sediments and mosquitoes but along the east coast lies the undersea canyon known as the Tongue Of The Ocean. The Tongue is over 5,000 feet deep and separates Andros from Nassau. A reef runs almost continuously along the Tongue off Andros. It is not, as some proclaim, a barrier reef. This of course doesn't matter much unless you're planning to do a single 100 mile long dive and will pout if there are any breaks in the reef.

The structure off Andros is considered mainly a fringing reef and there is great diving for much of its length. The wall that drops straight into the Tongue of the Ocean starts too deep for most dives and for most coral growth. There is a wide ledge that runs from the drop-off to another wall that rises straight up to about 70-80 feet. This "false wall" is a large mass of reef sliced with mini canyons. Inside the splits are thick black coral bushes and a multitude of sponges.

The best medium dives I've seen off Andros are on very large coral heads that rise about 30 feet off the sand. Anytime you can dive on big coral heads that are surrounded by sand make sure you do it. The heads act as magnets for every conceivable bit of life in the area. They make excellent night dives as well.

Andros is also famous for its Blue Holes. There are inland as well as tidal holes around the island. Most diving is done around the

Diver in pool of light

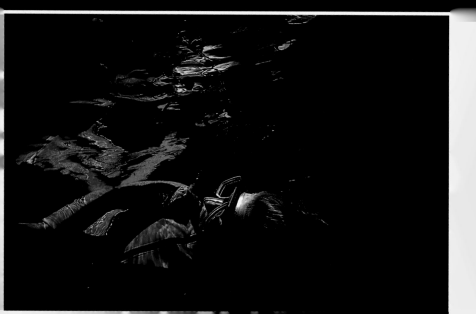

Under a ledge

Sponges

rims of these sink holes but there are special dives led as penetrations into caves leading off the main holes.

ELEUTHERA

Eleuthera is a long, narrow island that geographically includes Spanish Wells and Harbour Island. The one famous dive that I have to call by name is "current cut." This is a dive where you jump off the boat into a raging tidal current and fly over the reef. It's an easy dive as you never have to swim: the boat picks you up at the other end of the cut. The cut is populated and traversed by a lot of big fish that wait in the current for smaller creatures to be swept in with the tide. Other diving around Eleuthera includes several wrecks and blue holes.

LONG ISLAND

Long Island, specifically Stella Maris, has long been famous for its shark dive. When I saw this feeding it was done as a frenzy dive. The other dives around Long Island include an excellent group of large coral heads in about 45 feet of water. This area, Barracuda Head, has a resident school of Horse-eye Jacks and a sample of every kind of other marine life imaginable. It was a photographer's dream and I could spend a year diving around just those heads.

Conception Island is a day trip from Long Island and has walls as nice as anywhere I've seen. There are swim throughs that squirt you out over the wall, big black coral trees and giant orange elephant ears sponges.

SAN SALVADOR

San Salvador is known as the island where Columbus first got sand in his pointy shoes. National Geographic doesn't think so; Club Med does. Take your pick.

San Salvador is known for its walls, walls, walls. The walls start shallow and some areas have a more than vertical drop. There is loads of Black Coral and the possibilities for seeing anything swim by in the deep water.

CAY SAL

Cay Sal is an atoll with a few small, uninhabited bumps rising above the surface. It is separated from the main Bahama Plateau by deep water and good currents that combine to form the Gulf Stream. It's just north of Cuban waters and can only be visited by live-aboard.

Cay Sal has an wonderful stretch of wall off what is called the "Elbow" of Double-Headed Shot Cay. It starts in about 70 feet of water and has huge coral buttresses that spill out into the Blue.

Up against the low island of the Elbow is great shallow diving. The limestone island is riddled with caverns, some of which have open skylights. It is great for night dives as well. One small cavern I was inside was filled with at least 30 orange-ball corallimorphs.

Cay Sal also has several blue hole dives. One of them is filled with Sharpnose and Nurse Sharks which are fed by divemasters from the live-aboards.

EAST WALL OF THE PLATEAU

All along the edge of the Bahama Plateau, from east of Cay Sal and north back up to Bimini, is excellent, and rarely dived reef.

The Victories, Cat Cay and The Oranges are some of the known areas. The medium reef along here looks like just a flat sloping bottom but it is actually grown up at least 10 feet off the sand and intercut with crevices overflowing with sponges of every species.

Along here too is Tuna Alley where divers have seen giant Bluefin Tuna.

There is much more diving in The Bahamas then I have covered here. More than we could cover in our lifetimes. Hogsty Reef is an example of a rarely visited spot. It is a perfect little atoll in the middle of deep water in the Southern Bahamas.

A wonderful thing about The Bahamas is that even though it is the number one dive destination in the world, the dive areas are so plentiful and so widespread that you don't have to dive in a crowd. Even with the number of divers that visit each year, there are still great expanses of reef never seen by humans.

Some of the brightest colors on The Bahama reefs are sponges

Shallow cut

Growth on a sonar cable

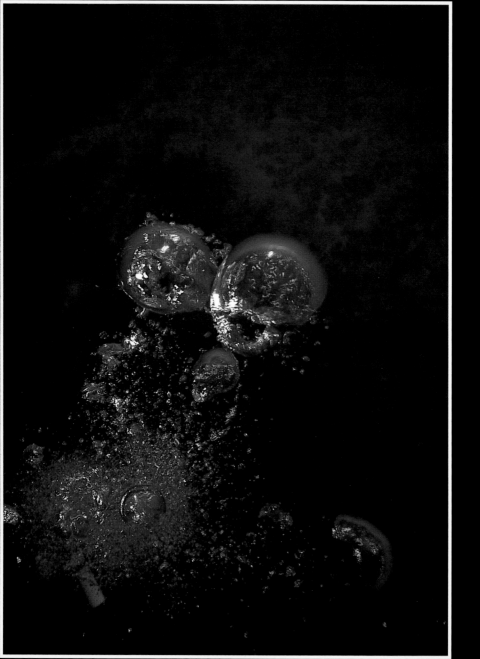

ABACO

Dive Abaco
P.O. Box 555
Marsh Harbour

809 367-2787

Hope Town Dive Shop
Hope Town, Abaco Harbour

809 366-0292

Walker's Cay Undersea Adventures
P.O. Box
Ft. Lauderdale

800 327-8150

ANDROS

Small Hope Bay
P.O. Box 21667
Ft. Lauderdale, FL 33335
800 223-6961
809 368-2014

BIMINI

Bimini Undersea Adventures
P.O. Box
Ft. Lauderdale, FL
800 348-4644
305 522-2011

ELEUTHERA

Romora Bay Club
P.O. Box 146
Harbour Island, Bahamas
809 333-2323

Valentine's Dive Center
3928 Shelbyville Road
Louisville, KY 40207
800 383-6480

EXUMA

Exuma Fantasea
P.O. Box 29261
George Town, Exuma, Bahamas
809 336-3483

LONG ISLAND

Stella Maris Inn
P.O. Box SM 105
Stella Maris, Long Island Bahamas
800 426-0466
809336-2106

SAN SALVADOR

Club Med
800 CLUB MED

Riding Rock Inn
750 SW 34th St, Suite 206
Ft. Lauderdale, FL 33315
800 272-1492
809 332-2631

GRAND BAHAMA

Underwater Explorers Society
UNEXSO
P.O. Box F-2433
Freeport, Grand Bahama
800 992-DIVE
809 373-1244

Sunn Odyssey Divers
Atlantik Beach Resort
P.O. Box F-4166
Freeport, Grand Bahama
809 373-1444

Xanadu Dive Center
P.O. Box F-2438
Freeport, Grand Bahama
800 336-0938
809 352-5856

NEW PROVIDENCE

Stuart Cove's
P.O. Box CB-11697
Nassau, Bahamas
800 879-9832
809 362-4171

Dive, Dive, Dive
P.O. Box N-8050
Nassau, Bahamas
800 328-8029
809 362-1143

Nassau Scuba Centre
P.O. Box 21766
Ft. Lauderdale, FL 33335
800 327-8150
809 362-1964

Sun Skiff Divers
P.O. Box N-142
Nassau, Bahamas
800 331-5884
809 362-1979

Bahama Divers
P.O. Box ss-5004
Nassau, Bahamas
809 393-5644

Divi Bahamas Beach Resort
2401 NW 34th Ave
Miami, FL 33142
800 367-3484
809 362-1964

Sun Divers
British Colonial Beach Resort
P.O. Box N-10728
Nassau, Bahamas
809 322-3301, ext 364

PARADISE ISLAND

Bahama Divers
P.O. Box SS-5004
Nassau, Bahamas
809 393-5644

LIVE-ABOARDS

Sea Fever Diving Cruises
P.O. Box 39-8276
Miami Beach, FL 33139
800 44-FEVER
800 330-1117 (FL)
305 531-DIVE

Bottom Time Adventures
P.O. Box 11919
Ft. Lauderdale, FL 33339
800 234-8464
305 561-0111

Blackbeard's Cruises
P.O. Box 661091
Miami Springs, FL 33266
800 327-9600
305 888-1226

Crown Cruise Line
P.O. Box 10265
Riviera Beach, FL 33419
800 841-7447

M/V Dream Too
P.O. Box 3271
Indiantlantic, FL 32903
407 723-9312

Sea Dragon 717
SW Coconut Dr.
Ft. Lauderdale, FL 33315
305 522-0161

OTHER SERVICES

Bahamas Tourist Office
800 327-7678

Bahamasair
800 222-4262

Innerspace Visions
Wild Dolphin Trips
305 669-0118

Bimini Big Game Fishing Club
and Hotel
809 347-2391

Compleat Angler, Bimini
809 347-3122

Green Turtle Club
Green Turtle Cay
809 365-4271

Conch Inn Resort and Marina
Marsh Harbour
809 367-2233

Lucayan Beach Resort and Casino
Grand Bahama
809 373-7777

Index

The author and publishers of Underwater Bahamas would
like to thank...

The People of The Bahamas
The Bahamian Government
Bahamas Tourist Office
Bahamasair

for their hospitality.

Also from Bob Friel and Novelty Publishing:
UNDERWATER MALDIVES

A journey in text and photos to the Republic of Maldives, an island nation in the Indian Ocean. Underwater Maldives is Mantas, Sharks, soft corals and more.

TO ORDER:
UNDERWATER MALDIVES, UNDERWATER BAHAMAS or to be included on our mailing list for trips and future publications, write to:

BLUE EDGE PUBLICATIONS
P.O. BOX 190213
Miami Beach, FL 33119
Phone/Fax: (305) 6734069

UNDERWATER BAHAMAS	(Hard Cover)	$24.95
	(Soft Cover)	$19.95
UNDERWATER MALDIVES	(Hard Cover)	$15.00

Send cheque or money order and please add $2.50 shipping and handling for each book.